Mischievous Multiplication & D

Paul Broadbent

CW00951719

In a hidden cave, far away in a magical land, lives a wise wizard, called Whimstaff. Every now and again, he searches for a young apprentice, so he can pass on his magical Maths powers. And this time, Whimstaff has chosen you!

Whimstaff shares the cave with a goblin and a little, red dragon. Pointy, the goblin, is very clever. The dragon, called Miss Snufflebeam, breathes small puffs of fire. She is clumsy and often loses the wizard's magical letters and numbers.

Pointy has two greedy, pet frogs, called Mugly and Bugly, who are very lazy and spend most of their time croaking, eating and sleeping. But every so often, they amaze Pointy by helping with an exercise!

Wizard Whimstaff and his friends are very happy in their cave, solving Maths problems. Join them on a magical quest to become a fully qualified Maths wizard!

★ Contents

2	Magnificent Multiplication	18	Gruesome Grouping
4	Fantastic Three	20	Terrific Trios
6	Marvellous Multiplication	22	Dazzling Division
8	Powerful Patterns	24	Revolting Remainders
10	Fascinating Facts	26	Tricky Ten
12	Tremendous Ten	28	Apprentice Wizard Challenge 2
14	Apprentice Wizard Challenge 1	30	Answers
16	Spellbound Sharing	32	Wizard's Certificate of Excellence

Letts

Magnificent Multiplication

I'm Miss Snufflebeam and I get very confused! Oh dear – I know the 2 times table, but now I need to learn the 4 times table!

Rabracadada! If you know the 2 times table, the 4 times table is easy! Just remember that 4 is double 2.

The answer to $3 \times \underline{4} = 12$ will be double the answer to $3 \times \underline{2} = 6$

Look at these.

$5 \times \underline{2} = 10$	$6 \times \underline{2} = 12$	$7 \times \underline{2} = 14$
$5 \times \underline{4} = 20$	$6 \times \underline{4} = 24$	$7 \times \underline{4} = 28$

The numbers in the 4 times table are always even numbers.

Task 1 Dabracababra! My spell has made the numbers appear. Can you complete the spell by casting a circle around the even numbers and then colouring the numbers in the 4 times table yellow?

1 2 3 4 5 6 7 8 9 10

11 12 13 14 15 16 17 18 19 20

21 22 23 24 25 26 27 28 29 30

31 32 33 34 35 36 37 38 39 40

Task 2 My head hurts! Can you write the answers and learn these facts?

a $1 \times 4 =$

b $2 \times 4 =$

c $3 \times 4 =$

d $4 \times 4 =$

e $5 \times 4 =$

f $6 \times 4 =$

g $7 \times 4 =$

h $8 \times 4 =$

i $9 \times 4 =$

j $10 \times 4 =$

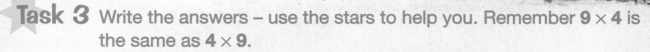

Task 3 Write the answers – use the stars to help you. Remember 9×4 is the same as 4×9.

a $5 \times 4 =$ ⬜

$4 \times 5 =$ ⬜

b $2 \times 4 =$ ⬜

$4 \times 2 =$ ⬜

c $7 \times 4 =$ ⬜

$4 \times 7 =$ ⬜

d $6 \times 4 =$ ⬜

$4 \times 6 =$ ⬜

e $3 \times 4 =$ ⬜

$4 \times 3 =$ ⬜

f $8 \times 4 =$ ⬜

$4 \times 8 =$ ⬜

Task 4 Join together pairs of clouds that have the same answer.

a 6×2

b 2×2

c 4×4

d 1×4

e 10×2

f 3×4

g 8×2

h 5×4

Sorcerer's Skill Check

Find the answers and then use the code to colour the stars.

a $9 \times 4 =$

b $4 \times 8 =$

c $3 \times 4 =$

d $4 \times 4 =$

e $5 \times 4 =$

f $2 \times 8 =$

g $2 \times 6 =$

h $4 \times 6 =$

i $10 \times 2 =$

36
32   16
20   12
24

Well completed, my apprentice! Add a gold star
to your certificate.

Fantastic Three

I'm Pointy, Wizard Whimstaff's clever assistant! He has 21 spellbooks and it's my job to look after them.

Sometimes Wizard Whimstaff likes 3 books in 7 piles.

 Sometimes Wizard Whimstaff likes 7 books in 3 rows.

7 lots of 3 = 21   7 × 3 = 21
3 lots of 7 = 21   3 × 7 = 21

Task 1 Write the answer for each of these. Remember that **2 × 3** has the same answer as **3 × 2**. You'll soon get the hang of it!

a 5 × 3 = ☐
   3 × 5 = ☐

b 4 × 3 = ☐
   3 × 4 = ☐

c 6 × 3 = ☐
   3 × 6 = ☐

d 3 × 3 = ☐

e 7 × 3 = ☐
   3 × 7 = ☐

f 8 × 3 = ☐
   3 × 8 = ☐

Task 2 Now you have a try! Draw wizard hats to show **2 × 3**. Super!

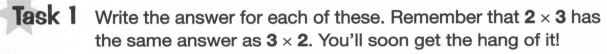

Task 3 Practice makes perfect! Write the answers and learn these facts.

a $1 \times 3 =$ ☐   **b** $2 \times 3 =$ ☐   **c** $3 \times 3 =$ ☐   **d** $4 \times 3 =$ ☐

e $5 \times 3 =$ ☐   **f** $6 \times 3 =$ ☐

g $7 \times 3 =$ ☐   **h** $8 \times 3 =$ ☐   **i** $9 \times 3 =$ ☐   **j** $10 \times 3 =$ ☐

Task 4 This is Wizard Whimstaff's favourite hat, but the ribbons came off when he was riding his broomstick! Help me to mend the hat by matching sums on the ribbons to the correct button answers.

a 4×3

d 9×3

b 3×3

e 8×3

c 6×3

f 5×3

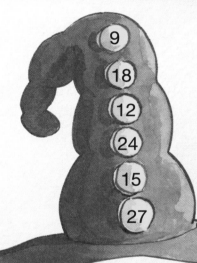

9
18
12
24
15
27

Sorcerer's Skill Check

These multiplication tables are difficult. I've started, but can you write the missing numbers? You'll soon get the hang of it!

a

×	3	2	5
2			10
3			
10			

b

×	3	10	2
5			
4		40	
6			

Another gold star! I wish I was as clever as you!

Marvellous Multiplication

We're Mugly and Bugly and we're here to give you a brain cell alert!

The 5 times table and the 10 times table are easy to learn.

Slurp! Look at the repeated pattern in these answers.

×5	5	10	15	20	25	30	35
×10	10	20	30	40	50	60	70

Task 1 These cauldrons multiply by 10 and 5. Write the numbers coming out. Burp! Wish we could multiply our dinner by 10!

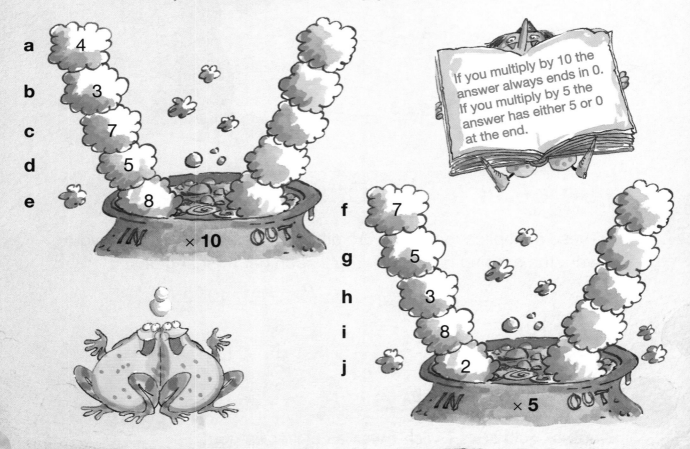

a 4
b 3
c 7
d 5
e 8

× 10

If you multiply by 10 the answer always ends in 0. If you multiply by 5 the answer has either 5 or 0 at the end.

f 7
g 5
h 3
i 8
j 2

× 5

6

Task 2 This is a job for Pointy! Slurp ... or you of course! Write the missing numbers.

a $3 \times 5 = $ ⬜

b $6 \times $ ⬜ $ = 30$

c $3 \times $ ⬜ $ = 15$

d $10 \times 9 = $ ⬜

e $2 \times 5 = $ ⬜

f ⬜ $ \times 10 = 40$

g $7 \times $ ⬜ $ = 70$

h ⬜ $ \times 3 = 30$

i ⬜ $ \times 10 = 100$

j $6 \times $ ⬜ $ = 60$

k $10 \times $ ⬜ $ = 80$

l $10 \times $ ⬜ $ = 10$

m ⬜ $ \times 4 = 20$

n $8 \times 5 = $ ⬜

o $5 \times $ ⬜ $ = 35$

p ⬜ $ \times 2 = 10$

q ⬜ $ \times 9 = 45$

r $5 \times 5 = $ ⬜

Sorcerer's Skill Check

You can find a route across this marvellous maze, if you know your 5 times table. Cast a circle around numbers in the 5 times table and you will get to the other side.

8	32	51	31	20	45	50	5	10	14	19	27	50	35	15	20	24	42	34
12	23	27	36	30	43	24	8	35	34	20	5	45	51	23	25	27	20	(10) → OUT
IN → (5) → (20)	46	10	5	34	15	25	20	31	30	38	22	27	19	30	16	35	12	
16	(25)	18	45	19	62	30	17	13	31	45	19	45	10	15	5	17	45	40
9	(50) → (15)	35	23	25	20	49	21	8	25	44	40	26	24	27	51	17	30	
16	31	42	46	6	45	18	48	20	30	40	23	30	22	10	15	25	33	45
13	9	17	8	4	40	15	20	25	39	29	28	25	20	5	41	5	35	50

You can now add your gold star to your certificate, young apprentice! Super!

Powerful Patterns

I'm Wizard Whimstaff! I love multiplication tables, as there are so many wonderful patterns.

Abracadabra! Each of the table toads jumps in different multiples.

Look at this number line.

0 1 2 3 4 5 6 7 8 9 10 11 12

8 is a multiple of both 2 and 4.

12 is a multiple of 2, 3 and 4.

Remember – multiples are numbers in a multiplication table.

Task 1 Now have a go at this exercise. Draw the toad jumps above each table, my apprentice.

a 2 times table

0 1 2 3 4 5 6 7 8 9 10 11 12 13 14 15 16 17 18 19 20

b 3 times table

0 1 2 3 4 5 6 7 8 9 10 11 12 13 14 15 16 17 18 19 20 21 22 23 24 25 26 27 28 29 30

c 4 times table

0 1 2 3 4 5 6 7 8 9 10 11 12 13 14 15 16 17 18 19 20 21 22 23 24 25 26 27 28 29 30 31 32 33 34 35 36 37 38 39 40

Task 2 Look at the number lines in Task 1 to help you answer these.

a Which numbers are multiples of 3 and 4? _____

b Which numbers are multiples of 2 and 3? _____

c Which numbers are multiples of 2 and 4? _____

d Which number is a multiple of 2, 3 and 4? _____

8

Task 3 Write the missing numbers on these lily pad patterns. Just do the best you can on the task. Abracadabra!

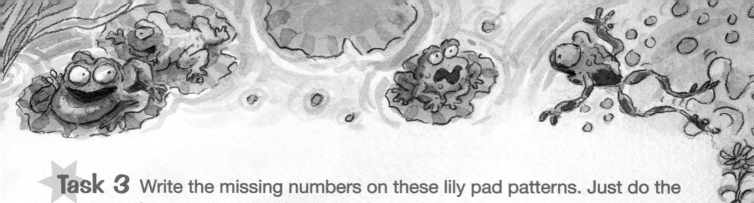

a ( ) ( ) (9) (12) (15) ( ) ( ) ( )

b (2) ( ) ( ) ( ) ( ) ( ) (14) (16)

c ( ) (20) (25) ( ) ( ) (40) ( ) ( )

d (8) (12) ( ) ( ) (24) ( ) ( ) ( )

Sorcerer's Skill Check

Hey Presto! Look at this tables square – it's quite magical!

Colour and write about any patterns you notice.

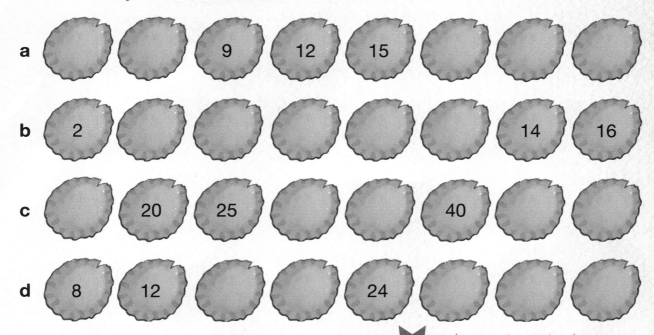

×	1	2	3	4	5
1	1	2	3	4	5
2	2	4	6	8	10
3	3	6	9	12	15
4	4	8	12	16	20
5	5	10	15	20	25

My magic patterns:

Cabradababa! Another gold star!

Fascinating Facts

Apprentice wizards need to
learn these multiplication tables:

× 2   × 3   × 4   × 5   × 10

3 × 6   2 × 7   4 × 5

Practice makes perfect!

Task 1 How quickly can you answer these, young apprentice? Write the
answer. Colour the star red if you knew the answer instantly. Super!

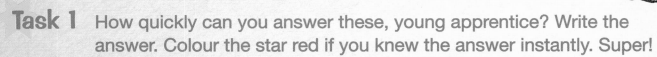

a 3 × 5 = ☆   **f** 4 × 4 = ☆   **k** 8 × 5 = ☆   **p** 9 × 3 = ☆

b 2 × 7 = ☆   **g** 6 × 5 = ☆   **l** 4 × 3 = ☆   **q** 7 × 4 = ☆

c 8 × 3 = ☆   **h** 2 × 9 = ☆   **m** 5 × 5 = ☆   **r** 2 × 3 = ☆

d 6 × 4 = ☆   **i** 10 × 8 = ☆   **n** 3 × 6 = ☆   **s** 5 × 7 = ☆

e 2 × 8 = ☆   **j** 9 × 4 = ☆   **o** 10 × 2 = ☆   **t** 9 × 5 = ☆

Task 2 I'm tidying up for Wizard Whimstaff. Help me by matching the
potion pots and jars with the same answer.

a 8 × 3   **b** 6 × 2   **c** 2 × 8   **d** 9 × 2

e 6 × 4   **f** 4 × 4   **g** 6 × 3   **h** 3 × 4

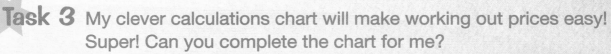

Task 3 My clever calculations chart will make working out prices easy! Super! Can you complete the chart for me?

item \ number	1	2	3	4	5	6	7	8	9	10
a										
b				12p						
c										
d							35p			

Task 4 Use my clever chart and write the answers for these. You'll soon get the hang of it!

a What is the cost of 5 🧪 and 3 🪄 ? _____p

b What is the cost of 6 🧹 and 5 🫕 ? _____p

c You have 20p. How many 🫕 could you buy? _____

d You have 30p. How many 🪄 could you buy? _____

Sorcerer's Skill Check

Here's a wizard idea! Time yourself to answer these. Write the answers on paper. Repeat and try to beat your previous time. Super!

a 5×5		**d** 6×3		**g** 2×4		**j** 8×2
b 7×3		**e** 10×7		**h** 3×4		**k** 9×10
c 4×7		**f** 5×8		**i** 10×4		**l** 10×10

Well completed, my apprentice! Give yourself a gold star.

Tremendous Ten

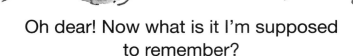

Oh dear! Now what is it I'm supposed to remember?

Cabradababa! Oh yes – when multiplying a number by 10, each digit moves one place to the left.

```
  H T U
 |  2 4 |  × 10

24 × 10  | 2 4 0 |
```

The number has become ten times bigger!

Task 1 Oh my head hurts! Can you multiply these numbers by 10?

a
```
  H T U
 |  3 2 |  × 10
```
32 × 10 | | | |

b
```
  H T U
 |  4 7 |  × 10
```
47 × 10 | | | |

c
```
  H T U
 |  6 1 |  × 10
```
61 × 10 | | | |

d
```
  H T U
 |  3 9 |  × 10
```
39 × 10 | | | |

e
```
  H T U
 |  8 4 |  × 10
```
84 × 10 | | | |

f
```
  H T U
 |  7 0 |  × 10
```
70 × 10 | | | |

Task 2 Dabracababra! My clumsy magic has made the answers disappear. Can you answer these?

a 18 × 10 =

b 42 × 10 =

c 89 × 10 =

d 50 × 10 =

e 33 × 10 =

f 21 × 10 =

g 97 × 10 =

h 19 × 10 =

| □ | □□□□□ | □□ | □□□□□ | □□□□ |

START ➡

	52 × 10	502 L	31 × 10	310 F	60 × 10	600 S	18 × 10
	520 A		330 O		61 W		180 I
61 × 10	870 C	87 × 10	807 S	33 × 10	800 D	84 × 10	340 L	34 × 10
610 H		104 F		210 T		840 V		43 N
93 × 10	930 E	14 × 10	140 S	21 × 10	72 L	62 × 10	620 E	51 × 10
FINISH	903 R		104 C		201 B		72 P		510 R
990 S	99 × 10	410 N	41 × 10	760 I	76 × 10	470 O	47 × 10	830 C	83 × 10

Sorcerer's Skill Check

These cauldrons multiply by 10. My head hurts! Will you write the missing numbers on the cauldrons for me?

a 27
b 31
c 94
d 63

e 370
f 920
g 630
h 190

× 10   OUT

× 10   OUT

Well done! Yet another gold star! Super!

13

Apprentice Wizard Challenge 1

⭐ **Challenge 1** Write the missing numbers.

a   8   12   20

b   9   12   15

c   15   25   30

⭐ **Challenge 2** Which facts do these stars show?

a

☐ × ☐ = ☐

☐ × ☐ = ☐

b

☐ × ☐ = ☐

☐ × ☐ = ☐

Remember, 2 × 6 is the same as 6 × 2.

⭐ **Challenge 3** Complete the grids.

a

×	3	10	2
5			
2			
3			

b

×	3	4	5
2			
10			
4			

⭐ **Challenge 4** Write the answers.

a 8 × 3 = ☐   b 7 × 4 = ☐   c 4 × 4 = ☐   d 5 × 7 = ☐

e 9 × 2 = ☐   f 3 × 6 = ☐   g 7 × 2 = ☐   h 10 × 2 = ☐

i 6 × 10 = ☐   j 5 × 3 = ☐   k 5 × 5 = ☐   l 6 × 5 = ☐

Challenge 5 Which numbers will come out of each of these hats?

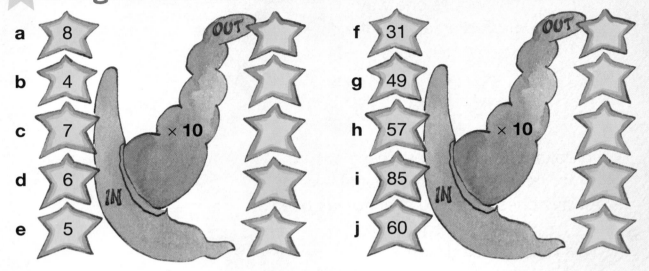

a 8
b 4
c 7 × 10
d 6
e 5

f 31
g 49
h 57 × 10
i 85
j 60

Challenge 6 Draw lines to join the potion bottles that have the same answers.

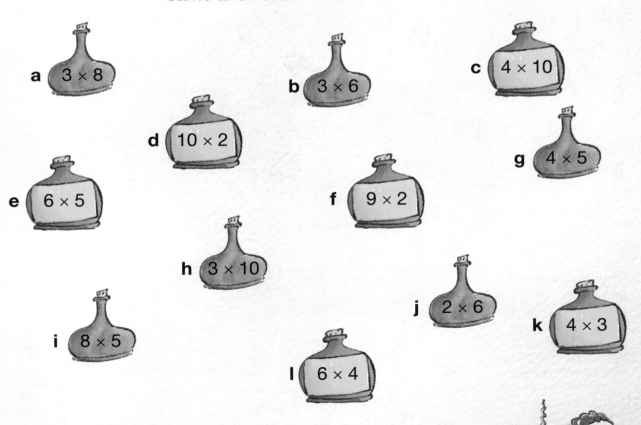

a 3 × 8

b 3 × 6

c 4 × 10

d 10 × 2

g 4 × 5

e 6 × 5

f 9 × 2

h 3 × 10

j 2 × 6

k 4 × 3

i 8 × 5

l 6 × 4

Excellent work, young apprentice! Add a gold star to your certificate!

Spellbound Sharing

Sharing is one way of dividing a quantity.

Allakazan! 12 cobweb cakes shared between 4 gives 3 each.
Always check that the sharing has been done equally.
This is the division sign ÷.   12 ÷ 4 = 3

Task 1   Work your magic to share these bottles of potions out equally on to the trays.

a

6 ÷ 2 = ☐

b

8 ÷ 4 = ☐

c

18 ÷ 3 = ☐

d

15 ÷ 5 = ☐

Task 2 Abracadabra! Draw cakes to show how many are on each plate and then write the answer.

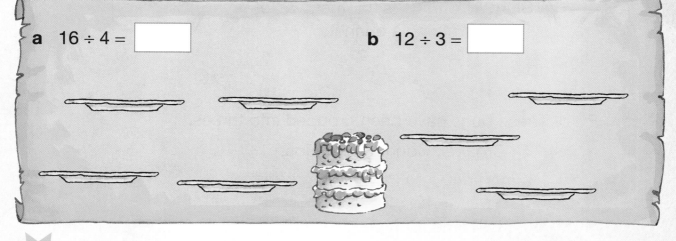

a $16 \div 4 =$ ☐   **b** $12 \div 3 =$ ☐

Task 3 Write the answer for each of these. Just do the best you can, young apprentice!

a $8 \div 2 =$ **b** $10 \div 5 =$ **c** $9 \div 3 =$ **d** $12 \div 2 =$

e $20 \div 10 =$ **f** $14 \div 2 =$ **g** $15 \div 3 =$ **h** $20 \div 5 =$

Sorcerer's Skill Check

Now colour the boxes by matching each answer to a colour on the code.

a $24 \div 3$ ☐   **f** $18 \div 3$ ☐

b $14 \div 2$ ☐   **g** $35 \div 5$ ☐

c $27 \div 3$ ☐   **h** $18 \div 2$ ☐

d $30 \div 5$ ☐   **i** $16 \div 2$ ☐

e $21 \div 3$ ☐   **j** $12 \div 2$ ☐

6   7
8   9

Grub's up! This is our way of sharing. We eat the food and you can have another gold star!

Gruesome Grouping

Slurp! Grouping is another way of dividing a quantity.

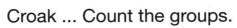

Burp! These bugs have been grouped into threes.

Croak ... Count the groups.

12 grouped into threes = <u>4</u> groups.

$12 \div 3 = \underline{4}$

Is it time for a snooze yet?

Task 1 Group these into threes and count the groups. Slurp! All these bugs are making us hungry.

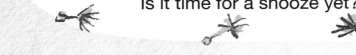

a $9 \div 3 =$ ☐   **b** $15 \div 3 =$ ☐

Task 2 Group these into fours and count the groups. Hurry up, before we have them for dinner!

 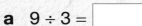  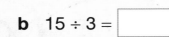

a $16 \div 4 =$ ☐   **b** $8 \div 4 =$ ☐

Task 3 Group these into twos and count the groups. Good, you have nearly finished – grub's up!

a $10 \div 2 =$ ☐   **b** $12 \div 2 =$ ☐

Task 4 Brain cell alert! Circle these to show the groups and then count the groups.

a 15 ÷ 3 = ☐

b 12 ÷ 4 = ☐

c 14 ÷ 2 = ☐

d 10 ÷ 5 = ☐

e 8 ÷ 2 = ☐

f 18 ÷ 3 = ☐

Sorcerer's Skill Check

Burp! Match each cobweb to the correct answer on the spider.

15 ÷ 3   1   8 ÷ 4   6   40 ÷ 5

10 ÷ 10   21 ÷ 3

2   7   8   10

5

18 ÷ 3   40 ÷ 10   50 ÷ 5

6 ÷ 2   18 ÷ 2

4   9   3

Rabracadada! You've got another gold star!

Terrific Trios

There's a super link between multiplication and division.

 5   3   15

$5 \times 3 = 15$ $15 \div 3 = 5$
$3 \times 5 = 15$ $15 \div 5 = 3$

We call numbers like these trios.
Multiplication and division facts can be made from their 'trios'.

Task 1   Now you have a try! Write the facts for these terrific trios. Super!

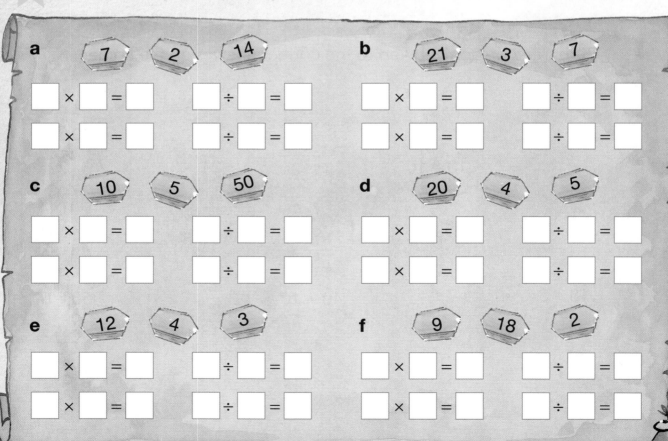

a   7   2   14

☐ × ☐ = ☐   ☐ ÷ ☐ = ☐
☐ × ☐ = ☐   ☐ ÷ ☐ = ☐

b   21   3   7

☐ × ☐ = ☐   ☐ ÷ ☐ = ☐
☐ × ☐ = ☐   ☐ ÷ ☐ = ☐

c   10   5   50

☐ × ☐ = ☐   ☐ ÷ ☐ = ☐
☐ × ☐ = ☐   ☐ ÷ ☐ = ☐

d   20   4   5

☐ × ☐ = ☐   ☐ ÷ ☐ = ☐
☐ × ☐ = ☐   ☐ ÷ ☐ = ☐

e   12   4   3

☐ × ☐ = ☐   ☐ ÷ ☐ = ☐
☐ × ☐ = ☐   ☐ ÷ ☐ = ☐

f   9   18   2

☐ × ☐ = ☐   ☐ ÷ ☐ = ☐
☐ × ☐ = ☐   ☐ ÷ ☐ = ☐

Task 2 Write the total score for these dice. Practice makes perfect!

a [ ] × 5 = [ ]

[ ] ÷ 5 = [ ]

b [ ] × 4 = [ ]

[ ] ÷ 4 = [ ]

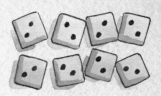

c [ ] × 2 = [ ]

[ ] ÷ 2 = [ ]

d [ ] × 4 = [ ]

[ ] ÷ 4 = [ ]

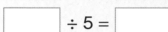

e [ ] × 5 = [ ]

[ ] ÷ 5 = [ ]

f [ ] × 3 = [ ]

[ ] ÷ 3 = [ ]

Sorcerer's Skill Check

Work your magic and colour the triangles with an even answer to find a path across the maze.

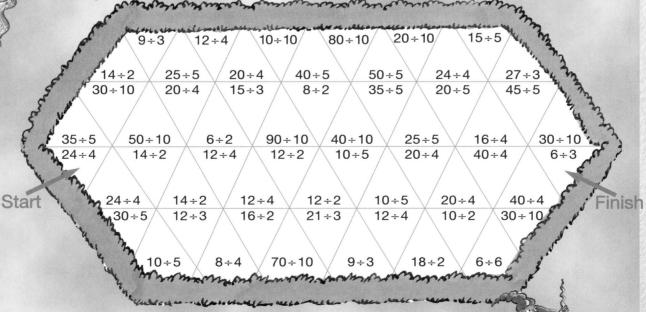

Another gold star! Well done!

Dazzling Division

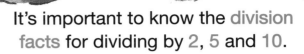

It's important to know the division facts for dividing by 2, 5 and 10.

Dividing by 3 and 4 are the other facts to try and learn.

Hey Presto! Look at these table facts to help you learn division facts.

$21 \div 3$	$\longrightarrow$	$3 \times$	7	$= 21$
$16 \div 4$	$\longrightarrow$	$4 \times$	4	$= 16$
$24 \div 4$	$\longrightarrow$	$4 \times$	6	$= 24$

Task 1 Write the answers and learn the division facts for 3 by heart. Do not worry if it seems hard at first, my apprentice.

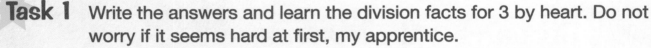

a $3 \div 3 =$ **b** $6 \div 3 =$ **c** $9 \div 3 =$

d $12 \div 3 =$ **e** $15 \div 3 =$ **f** $18 \div 3 =$ **g** $21 \div 3 =$

h $24 \div 3 =$ **i** $27 \div 3 =$ **j** $30 \div 3 =$

Task 2 Now write the answers and learn the division facts for 4 by heart. Just do the best you can.

a $4 \div 4 =$ **b** $8 \div 4 =$ **c** $12 \div 4 =$

d $16 \div 4 =$ **e** $20 \div 4 =$ **f** $24 \div 4 =$ **g** $28 \div 4 =$

h $32 \div 4 =$ **i** $36 \div 4 =$ **j** $40 \div 4 =$

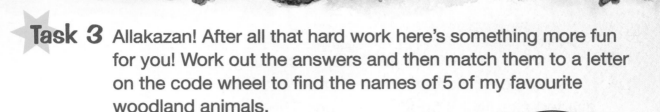

Task 3
Allakazan! After all that hard work here's something more fun for you! Work out the answers and then match them to a letter on the code wheel to find the names of 5 of my favourite woodland animals.

a $12 \div 3 = \boxed{}$ —— b $35 \div 5 = \boxed{}$ ——

$40 \div 5 = \boxed{}$ —— $40 \div 4 = \boxed{}$ ——

$16 \div 2 = \boxed{}$ —— $20 \div 2 = \boxed{}$ ——

$60 \div 10 = \boxed{}$ —— $40 \div 5 = \boxed{}$ ——

$18 \div 3 = \boxed{}$ —— e $25 \div 5 = \boxed{}$ ——

c $18 \div 2 = \boxed{}$ —— $16 \div 2 = \boxed{}$ ——

$6 \div 3 = \boxed{}$ —— d $30 \div 5 = \boxed{}$ —— $16 \div 4 = \boxed{}$ ——

$16 \div 4 = \boxed{}$ —— $4 \div 2 = \boxed{}$ —— $3 \div 3 = \boxed{}$ ——

$5 \div 5 = \boxed{}$ —— $18 \div 2 = \boxed{}$ —— $24 \div 3 = \boxed{}$ ——

$24 \div 3 = \boxed{}$ —— $36 \div 4 = \boxed{}$ —— $50 \div 10 = \boxed{}$ ——

$12 \div 2 = \boxed{}$ —— $30 \div 10 = \boxed{}$ —— $28 \div 4 = \boxed{}$ ——

$50 \div 5 = \boxed{}$ —— $5 \div 5 = \boxed{}$ ——

Sorcerer's Skill Check

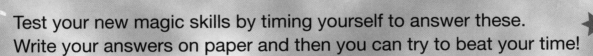

Test your new magic skills by timing yourself to answer these.
Write your answers on paper and then you can try to beat your time!

a $30 \div 10 =$ b $16 \div 4 =$ c $8 \div 2 =$ d $21 \div 3 =$

e $70 \div 10 =$ f $35 \div 5 =$ g $18 \div 3 =$ h $24 \div 4 =$

i $18 \div 2 =$ j $12 \div 4 =$ k $15 \div 3 =$ l $25 \div 5 =$

**Hurry up and add this gold star to your certificate.
Grub's up!**

Revolting Remainders

Slurp … have you heard about revolting remainders? Sometimes a number can't be divided exactly by another number. The number left over is called the remainder.
Croak ... What is 17 divided by 3?

$17 \div 3 = 5$ remainder 2.
Check by multiplying:
$5 \times 3 = 15 + 2 = 17$
$17 \div 3 = 5 \text{ r } 2$

Task 1 Draw circles to group the spiders and write the answers below. We've done one for you, but we'll let you do the rest!

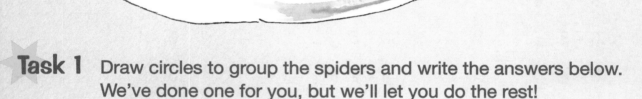

$15 \div 2 = 7$ remainder $\boxed{1}$

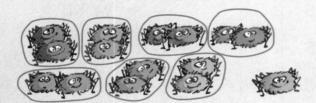

a $13 \div 2 = $ ☐

remainder ☐

b $14 \div 4 = $ ☐

remainder ☐

c $11 \div 5 = $ ☐

remainder ☐

d $10 \div 3 = $ ☐

remainder ☐

e $14 \div 3 = $ ☐

remainder ☐

f $10 \div 4 = $ ☐

remainder ☐

Task 2 This is a job for Pointy … or you of course! We're off for a snooze!
Write the answer with a remainder for each of these.

a 23 ÷ 3 = [ ] remainder [ ]   h 18 ÷ 4 = [ ] remainder [ ]

b 17 ÷ 2 = [ ] remainder [ ]   i 27 ÷ 4 = [ ] remainder [ ]

c 34 ÷ 10 = [ ] remainder [ ]   j 29 ÷ 3 = [ ] remainder [ ]

d 22 ÷ 4 = [ ] remainder [ ]   k 30 ÷ 4 = [ ] remainder [ ]

e 16 ÷ 3 = [ ] remainder [ ]   l 19 ÷ 2 = [ ] remainder [ ]

f 39 ÷ 5 = [ ] remainder [ ]   m 66 ÷ 10 = [ ] remainder [ ]

g 23 ÷ 4 = [ ] remainder [ ]   n 19 ÷ 3 = [ ] remainder [ ]

Sorcerer's Skill Check

We're happy when there are leftovers! Work these out and join them
to the correct remainders. Can you find the odd bottle?

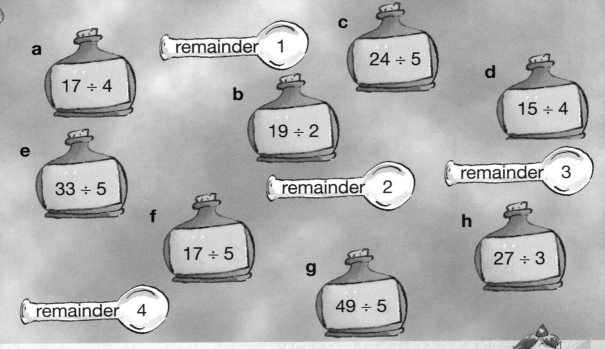

a 17 ÷ 4

remainder 1

c 24 ÷ 5

d 15 ÷ 4

b 19 ÷ 2

e 33 ÷ 5

remainder 2

remainder 3

f 17 ÷ 5

h 27 ÷ 3

g 49 ÷ 5

remainder 4

**Another gold star! You will be as clever as me soon!
Super!**

Tricky Ten

Oh dear – dividing makes me dizzy!
Dividing a number by 10 is easy though.
Just remember that each digit of the number moves one place to the right. Dabracababra!

H	T	U
2	7	0	$\div 10$

$270 \div 10 =$

	2	7

This is how it works.
The 200 becomes ten times smaller: 20
The 70 becomes ten times smaller: 7

Task 1   My head hurts! Can you divide these numbers by 10?

a
H	T	U
4	3	0

$430 \div 10 =$ ▢▢▢

b
H	T	U
1	9	0

$190 \div 10 =$ ▢▢▢

c
H	T	U
2	1	0

$210 \div 10 =$ ▢▢▢

d
H	T	U
3	0	0

$300 \div 10 =$ ▢▢▢

e
H	T	U
5	8	0

$580 \div 10 =$ ▢▢▢

f
H	T	U
7	3	0

$730 \div 10 =$ ▢▢▢

Task 2   You've done well! Rabracadada! I bet you find writing the answers for these easy, too.

a $320 \div 10 =$ ▢   **b** $440 \div 10 =$ ▢   **c** $790 \div 10 =$ ▢

d $110 \div 10 =$ ▢   **e** $640 \div 10 =$ ▢

f $720 \div 10 =$ ▢   **g** $350 \div 10 =$ ▢   **h** $520 \div 10 =$ ▢

Task 3 Colour these so that each star matches the moon with its answer.

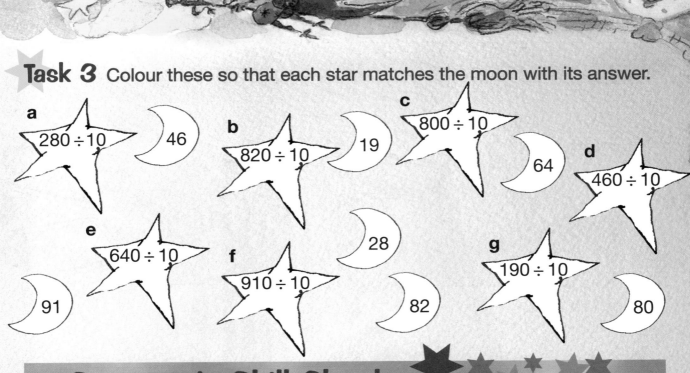

a $280 \div 10$ — 46

b $820 \div 10$ — 19

c $800 \div 10$ — 64

d $460 \div 10$

e $640 \div 10$ — 28

f $910 \div 10$ — 82

g $190 \div 10$ — 80

91

Sorcerer's Skill Check

Oops! These special wands divide by 10. I had better not use them with my clumsy skills, so write the missing numbers.

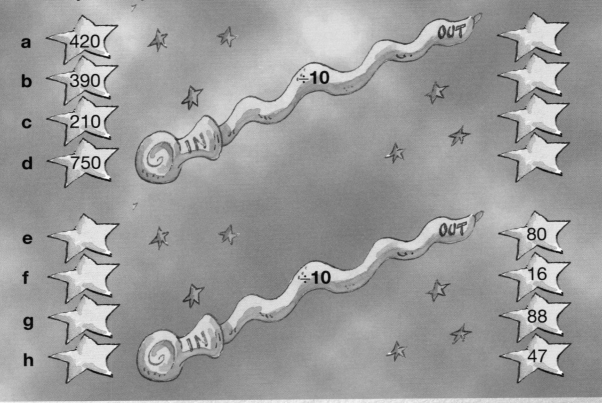

a 420

b 390

c 210

d 750

$\div 10$ OUT   IN

e

f

g

h

$\div 10$ OUT   IN

80

16

88

47

Is it time for a snooze yet? Even you will be ready for a snooze soon, but give yourself a gold star first!

Apprentice Wizard Challenge 2

Challenge 1 Draw lines to share these out equally and then write the answers.

a

$12 \div 3 =$ ▭

b

$10 \div 2 =$ ▭

Challenge 2 Group these and write how many groups there are.

a $15 \div 3 =$ ▭

b $18 \div 2 =$ ▭

c $15 \div 5 =$ ▭

Challenge 3 Write the facts for these trios.

a 4 24 6   **b** 16 2 8

▭ × ▭ = ▭   ▭ ÷ ▭ = ▭   ▭ × ▭ = ▭   ▭ ÷ ▭ = ▭

▭ × ▭ = ▭   ▭ ÷ ▭ = ▭   ▭ × ▭ = ▭   ▭ ÷ ▭ = ▭

Challenge 4 Answer these.

a 21 ÷ 3 =

b 16 ÷ 4 =

c 27 ÷ 3 =

d 18 ÷ 2 =

e 35 ÷ 5 =

f 14 ÷ 2 =

g 90 ÷ 10 =

h 28 ÷ 4 =

i 24 ÷ 3 =

j 36 ÷ 4 =

k 2 ÷ 2 =

l 70 ÷ 10 =

Challenge 5 Write the missing numbers for each magic wand.

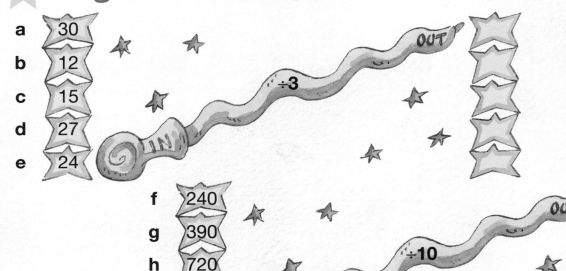

a 30
b 12
c 15
d 27
e 24

÷3 OUT

f 240
g 390
h 720
i 610
j 480

÷10 OUT

Challenge 6 Answer these.

a 23 ÷ 3 = remainder

b 31 ÷ 5 = remainder

c 35 ÷ 4 = remainder

d 17 ÷ 4 = remainder

e 28 ÷ 3 = remainder

f 22 ÷ 4 = remainder

You can now put your final gold star on your certificate! Dabacababra!

Answers

Pages 2–3

Task 1 circled even numbers:
2, 4, 6, 8, 10, 12, 14, 16, 18, 20, 22, 24, 26, 28, 30, 32, 34, 36, 38, 40
yellow numbers:
4, 8, 12, 16, 20, 24, 28, 32, 36, 40

Task 2
a 4
b 8
c 12
d 16
e 20
f 24
g 28
h 32
i 36
j 40

Task 3
a 20
  20
b 8
  8
c 28
  28
d 24
  24
e 12
  12
f 32
  32

Task 4
a 12 $6 \times 2 \rightarrow 3 \times 4$
b 4 $2 \times 2 \rightarrow 1 \times 4$
c 16 $4 \times 4 \rightarrow 8 \times 2$
d 4 $4 \times 1 \rightarrow 2 \times 2$
e 20 $10 \times 2 \rightarrow 5 \times 4$
f 12 $3 \times 4 \rightarrow 6 \times 2$
g 16 $8 \times 2 \rightarrow 4 \times 4$
h 20 $5 \times 4 \rightarrow 10 \times 2$

Sorcerer's Skill Check
a $9 \times 4 = 36$ green
b $4 \times 8 = 32$ red
c $3 \times 4 = 12$ blue
d $4 \times 4 = 16$ yellow
e $5 \times 4 = 20$ purple
f $2 \times 8 = 16$ yellow
g $2 \times 6 = 12$ blue
h $4 \times 6 = 24$ orange
i $10 \times 2 = 20$ purple

Pages 4–5

Task 1
a 15
  15
b 12
  12
c 18
  18
d 9
e 21
  21
f 24
  24

Task 2 Check your child has drawn 2 lots of 3 hats or 3 lots of 2 hats.

Task 3
a 3
b 6
c 9
d 12
e 15
f 18
g 21
h 24
i 27
j 30

Task 4
a 12
b 9
c 18
d 27
e 24
f 15

Sorcerer's Skill Check
a 6   4   10
  9   6   15
  30   20   50
b 15   50   10
  12   40   8
  18   60   12

Pages 6–7

Task 1
a 40
b 30
c 70
d 50
e 80
f 35
g 25
h 15
i 40
j 10

Task 2
a 15
b 5
c 5
d 90
e 10
f 4
g 10
h 10
i 10
j 10
k 8
l 1
m 5
n 40
o 7
p 5
q 5
r 25

Sorcerer's Skill Check
Check that your child has only circled numbers ending in 5 or 0.

Pages 8–9

Task 1 The jumps drawn by your child should match these:
a 2, 4, 6, 8, 10, 12, 14, 16, 18, 20
b 3, 6, 9, 12, 15, 18, 21, 24, 27, 30
c 4, 8, 12, 16, 20, 24, 28, 32, 36, 40

Task 2 Your child may include extra numbers – check they are correct.
a 12 24
b 6 12 18
c 4 8 12 16 20
d 12

Task 3
a 3 6 9 12 15 18 21 24
b 2 4 6 8 10 12 14 16
c 15 20 25 30 35 40 45 50
d 8 12 16 20 24 28 32 36

Sorcerer's Skill Check
Check your child's colouring. There are many possible answers.

Pages 10–11

Task 1
a 15
b 14
c 24
d 24
e 16
f 16
g 30
h 18
i 80
j 36
k 40
l 12
m 25
n 18
o 20
p 27
q 28
r 6
s 35
t 45

Task 2 a → e, b → h, c → f, d → g

Task 3
a 2p 4p 6p 8p 10p
  12p 14p 16p 18p 20p
b 3p 6p 9p 12p 15p
  18p 21p 24p 27p 30p
c 4p 8p 12p 16p 20p
  24p 28p 32p 36p 40p
d 5p 10p 15p 20p 25p
  30p 35p 40p 45p 50p

Task 4
a 22p
b 45p
c 6
d 7

Sorcerer's Skill Check
a 25
b 21
c 28
d 18
e 70
f 40
g 8
h 12
i 40
j 16
k 90
l 100

Pages 12–13

Task 1
a 320
b 470
c 610
d 390
e 840
f 700

Task 2
a 180
b 420
c 890
d 500
e 330
f 210
g 970
h 190

Task 3 A CHEST OF SILVER COINS

Sorcerer's Skill Check
a 270
b 310
c 940
d 630
e 37
f 92
g 63
h 19

Pages 14–15

Challenge 1
a 8 12 16 20 24 28 32
b 3 6 9 12 15 18 21
c 5 10 15 20 25 30 35

Challenge 2
a $3 \times 4 = 12$
  $4 \times 3 = 12$
b $4 \times 5 = 20$
  $5 \times 4 = 20$

Challenge 3
a 15 50 10
  6 20 4
  9 30 6
b 6 8 10
  30 40 50
  12 16 20

Challenge 4
a 24
b 28
c 16
d 35
e 18
f 18
g 14
h 20
i 60
j 15
k 25
l 30

Challenge 5
a 80
b 40
c 70
d 60
e 50
f 310
g 490
h 570
i 850
j 600

Challenge 6
a $3 \times 8 \rightarrow$ l 6×4
b $3 \times 6 \rightarrow$ f 9×2
c $4 \times 10 \rightarrow$ i 8×5
d $10 \times 2 \rightarrow$ g 4×5
e $6 \times 5 \rightarrow$ h 3×10
j $2 \times 6 \rightarrow$ k 4×3

Pages 16–17

Task 1
a 3
b 2
c 6
d 3

Task 2
a 4
b 4

Task 3
a 4
b 2
c 3
d 6
e 2
f 7
g 5
h 4

Sorcerer's Skill Check
a 8 green
b 7 red
c 9 yellow
d 6 blue
e 7 red
f 6 blue
g 7 red
h 9 yellow
i 8 green
j 6 blue

30

Task 1 **a** 3   **b** 5

Task 2 **a** 4   **b** 2

Task 3 **a** 5   **b** 6

Task 4 **a** 5   **d** 2
        b 3   **e** 4
        c 7   **f** 6

Sorcerer's Skill Check

$18 \div 3 \to 6$ $15 \div 3 \to 5$
$6 \div 2 \to 3$ $10 \div 10 \to 1$
$40 \div 10 \to 4$ $8 \div 4 \to 2$
$18 \div 2 \to 9$ $21 \div 3 \to 7$
$50 \div 5 \to 10$ $40 \div 5 \to 8$

Pages 20–21

Task 1 **a** $7 \times 2 = 14$ $14 \div 2 = 7$
        $2 \times 7 = 14$ $14 \div 7 = 2$
     b $3 \times 7 = 21$ $21 \div 3 = 7$
        $7 \times 3 = 21$ $21 \div 7 = 3$
     c $10 \times 5 = 50$ $50 \div 5 = 10$
        $5 \times 10 = 50$ $50 \div 10 = 5$
     d $4 \times 5 = 20$ $20 \div 5 = 4$
        $5 \times 4 = 20$ $20 \div 4 = 5$
     e $4 \times 3 = 12$ $12 \div 3 = 4$
        $3 \times 4 = 12$ $12 \div 4 = 3$
     f $9 \times 2 = 18$ $18 \div 2 = 9$
        $2 \times 9 = 18$ $18 \div 9 = 2$

Task 2 **a** 5   25   **d** 7   28
       25   5   28   7
     b 6   24   **e** 6   30
       24   6   30   6
     c 8   16   **f** 6   18
       16   8   18   6

Sorcerer's Skill Check

Check that the triangles coloured follow this path of sums:
$24 \div 4 = 6$, $18 \div 3 = 6$, $30 \div 5 = 6$,
$10 \div 5 = 2$, $12 \div 3 = 4$, $8 \div 4 = 2$,
$16 \div 2 = 8$, $20 \div 2 = 10$, $12 \div 2 = 6$,
$30 \div 3 = 10$, $10 \div 5 = 2$, $40 \div 10 = 4$,
$8 \div 2 = 4$, $40 \div 5 = 8$, $80 \div 10 = 8$,
$50 \div 5 = 10$, $20 \div 10 = 2$, $24 \div 4 = 6$,
$20 \div 5 = 4$, $16 \div 4 = 4$, $40 \div 4 = 10$,
$4 \div 2 = 2$, $6 \div 3 = 2$

Pages 22–23

Task 1 **a** 1   **f** 6
     b 2   **g** 7
     c 3   **h** 8
     d 4   **i** 9
     e 5   **j** 10

Task 2 **a** 1   **f** 6
     b 2   **g** 7
     c 3   **h** 8
     d 4   **i** 9
     e 5   **j** 10

Task 3 **a** 4 D   **d** 6 R
       8 E   2 A
       8 E   9 B
       6 R   9 B
                  3 I
     b 7 O   10 T
      10 T
      10 T   **e** 5 H
       8 E   8 E
       6 R   4 D
                  1 G
     c 9 B   8 E
       2 A   5 H
       4 D   7 O
       1 G   1 G
       8 E
       6 R

Sorcerer's Skill Check

   a 3   **g** 6
   b 4   **h** 6
   c 4   **i** 9
   d 7   **j** 3
   e 7   **k** 5
   f 7   **l** 5

Pages 24–25

Task 1 **a** 6 remainder 1
     b 3 remainder 2
     c 2 remainder 1
     d 3 remainder 1
     e 4 remainder 2
     f 2 remainder 2

Task 2 **a** 7 remainder 2
     b 8 remainder 1
     c 3 remainder 4
     d 5 remainder 2
     e 5 remainder 1
     f 7 remainder 4
     g 5 remainder 3
     h 4 remainder 2
     i 6 remainder 3
     j 9 remainder 2
     k 7 remainder 2
     l 9 remainder 1
     m 6 remainder 6
     n 6 remainder 1

Sorcerer's Skill Check

   a $17 \div 4 \to 4$ r 1
   b $19 \div 2 \to 9$ r 1
   c $24 \div 5 \to 4$ r 4
   d $15 \div 4 \to 3$ r 3
   e $33 \div 5 \to 6$ r 3
   f $17 \div 5 \to 3$ r 2
   g $49 \div 5 \to 9$ r 4
   h $27 \div 3 \to 9$
      this is the odd pot – there is no remainder!

Pages 26–27

Task 1 **a** 43   **d** 30
     b 19   **e** 58
     c 21   **f** 73

Task 2 **a** 32   **e** 64
     b 44   **f** 72
     c 79   **g** 35
     d 11   **h** 52

Task 3 Check that your child has coloured these to match
   a $280 \div 10 \to 28$
   b $820 \div 10 \to 82$
   c $800 \div 10 \to 80$
   d $460 \div 10 \to 46$
   e $640 \div 10 \to 64$
   f $910 \div 10 \to 91$
   g $190 \div 10 \to 19$

Sorcerer's Skill Check

   a 42   **e** 800
   b 39   **f** 160
   c 21   **g** 880
   d 75   **h** 470

Pages 28–29

Challenge 1
   a 4   **b** 5

Challenge 2
   a 5   **c** 3
   b 9

Challenge 3
   a $4 \times 6 = 24$ $24 \div 6 = 4$
       $6 \times 4 = 24$ $24 \div 4 = 6$
   b $2 \times 8 = 16$ $16 \div 8 = 2$
       $8 \times 2 = 16$ $16 \div 2 = 8$

Challenge 4
   a 7   **g** 9
   b 4   **h** 7
   c 9   **i** 8
   d 9   **j** 9
   e 7   **k** 1
   f 7   **l** 7

Challenge 5
   a 10   **f** 24
   b 4   **g** 39
   c 5   **h** 72
   d 9   **i** 61
   e 8   **j** 48

Challenge 6
   a 7 remainder 2
   b 6 remainder 1
   c 8 remainder 3
   d 4 remainder 1
   e 9 remainder 1
   f 5 remainder 2

Wizard's Certificate of Excellence

Magnificent Multiplication

Spellbound Sharing

Fantastic Three

Gruesome Grouping

Marvellous Multiplication

Terrific Trios

Powerful Patterns

Dazzling Division

Fascinating Facts

Revolting Remainders

Tremendous Ten

Tricky Ten

Apprentice Wizard Challenge 1

Apprentice Wizard Challenge 2

This is to state that Wizard Whimstaff awards

Apprentice —————————————

the title of Maths Wizard. Congratulations!

Wizard Whimstaff

Published 2002
10 9 8 7

Letts Educational, The Chiswick Centre,
414 Chiswick High Road, London W4 5TF
Tel 0845 602 1937   Fax 020 8742 8767
Email mail@lettsed.co.uk
www.Letts-SuccessZone.com

Text, design and illustrations © Letts Educational Ltd 2002

Author: Paul Broadbent
Book Concept and Development:
Helen Jacobs, Publishing Director; Sophie London, Project Editor
Design and Editorial: Cambridge Publishing Management Ltd.
Illustrations: Mike Phillips and Neil Chapman (Beehive Illustration)
Cover Illustration: Neil Chapman
Cover Design: Linda Males

Letts Educational is a division of Granada Learning Limited,
part of Granada plc

All rights reserved. No part of this publication may be reproduced,
stored in a retrieval system, or transmitted, in any form or by any
means, electronic, mechanical, photocopying, recording or otherwise,
without the prior permission of Letts Educational.

British Library Cataloguing in Publication Data
A CIP record for this book is available from the British Library.
ISBN 1 84315 098 0
Printed in Italy
Colour reproduction by PDQ Digital Media Solutions Ltd, Bungay, Suffolk